THE JOY

OF

GROWING OLD WITH GOD

YAV PUBLICATIONS
ASHEVILLE, NORTH CAROLINA

Copyright © 2012 Teri Pizza

All rights reserved. No part of this book shall be reproduced or transmitted in any form or by any means, electronic, mechanical, magnetic, photographic including photocopying, recording or by any information storage and retrieval system, without prior written permission of the publisher. No patent liability is assumed with respect to the use of the information contained herein. Although every precaution has been taken in the preparation of this book, the publisher and author assume no responsibility for errors or omissions. Neither is any liability assumed or damages resulting from the use of the information contained herein.

First Edition

ISBN: 978-1-937449-14-8

Published by:

YAV PUBLICATIONS
ASHEVILLE, NORTH CAROLINA

YAV books may be purchased in bulk for
educational, business, or promotional use.
Contact Books@yav.com or phone toll-free 888-693-9365.
Visit our website: www.InterestingWriting.com

Cover art and interior illustrations by Vern Hippensteal
www.VernHippensteal.com

3 5 7 9 10 8 6 4 2

Assembled in the United States of America
Published July 2012

ACKNOWLEDGEMENTS

The authors thank all those who have been part of our worldly walk but especially God who transforms us from the concerns of the world into a joyous people who embrace each new day as we journey to His heavenly Kingdom.

In this endeavor, we also thank all members of the Manuscript Committee: Rev. Alta Chase Raper, Chairman, Rev. Ron Lukat, Assistant Chair, and our typists and proofreaders, B. J. Byars, Jackie Cobb, and Janet Gullo.

We are especially grateful for the artistry of Vern Hippensteal who has lent us not only the cover art but also renderings from two of his other pieces, reproduced here in black and white with two of his poems.

Thanks need to be expressed to those who have directed and supported this project in so many ways: to our friends and families who prayed and offered monetary support toward the production of this book, we are most humbly thankful; to the families of our deceased contributors for graciously allowing us the privilege to read and reprint their loved ones' written works, to Kenton Temple, director of Anna Porter Library in Gatlinburg for advice and meeting space, to the Gatlinburg Presbyterian Church for meeting space, to attorney Joe G. Bagwell, to artist Claudette Pridemore for her valuable assistance with regard to our cover art, and, of course, to our publisher, Chris Yavelow, InterestingWriting.com.

O give thanks unto the LORD; for he is good; for his mercy endureth forever.

1 Chronicles 16:34 (KJV).

Teri Pizza, Project Coordinator for
The Joy of Growing Old with God

TABLE OF CONTENTS

Foreword 1

Lucy Neeley Adams 3
    Remembering My Daddy –
        Wadsworth Burnside Neeley 5
    Remembering My Mother –
        Louise Bennett Neeley 9

Marvel G. Adams 13
    The Father's House 15
    Consolation... 17
    My Home 19

Woody A. Adams.. 21
    Safely Back Home 23

Margie Bender 25
    Renewed Faith 27

Jackie Cobb 29
    Side By Side.. 31

Wayne Freeman.. 35
    Why Do We Live? 37

Vern Hippensteal...................................... 41
    Abram's Falls 43
    The Angel Oak 45

Ron Lukat.. 47
    Old Age is Not for the Weak..................... 49

Teri Pizza 55

Re: God 57

God's Gift 59

Alta Chase Raper 63

The Pastor's Ponderings
of June 20, 2004.................................65

The Pastor's Ponderings
of July 16, 2006.................................67

The Pastor's Ponderings
of May 2, 2010...................................71

The Pastor's Ponderings
of January 8, 2012.............................75

Helen Hughes Rice.......................................77

Through it All... 79

Who Am I? Where Have I Been? 81

Nancy Richards...83

But the Righteous Will Live By His Faith...85

H. Alvin Sharpe 89

Ten Talbas'a 91

Meditation at "Jacob's Chair".....................93

Meditation at the Tomb of
the Unknown Soldier 95

Faye Jean Warriner......................................97

Bedtime Thoughts..99

Index by Title..101

FOREWORD

Over the last twenty years the median age of America has increased 4.3% to 37.2 years old as of 2012. Those between forty-five and sixty-four now compose 26.4% of the population. America is aging at a rapid rate and more and more people are assessing what this means for their life. With the average retirement age in America being sixty-two, many Americans have over eighteen years to contemplate the meaning of their retirement and "senior years."

This book, *The Joy of Growing Old with God*, captures the reflections of several people who have found joy in the aging process. The authors wanted to provide a story that would encourage and inspire their children, their children's children, and others of the joys they were experiencing as they passed through this time in their life. An AARP Magazine article, "The Good Life" stated, "The older you are, the more likely you are to value religion, says a new Pew Research Center survey, 'Growing Old in America'." The authors in this book found this to be the case in their lives and therefore chose to focus their reflections on how their relationship with God has influenced their perspective of these years. Their stories grow out of their eyewitness accounts and experiences that they hope others will find meaningful.

These authors believe that age strips away the pretense of younger years and leaves bare the soul that is happily ready to listen to its Lord and Master. Even though the latter years may be filled with some medical issues and other challenges, these authors believe that their lives now are bigger, better, and more profound than they were when they were younger. Through these letters, poems, testimonials, and essays, they share the spirit and enthusiasm they have for life with God in their later years.

Any profits from this book over the costs of publishing will be donated to public libraries for the purchase of children's religious storybooks.

—Rev. Ronald Lukat
Gatlinburg Presbyterian Church

Lucy Neeley Adams

Year of birth: 1934
Age at writing: 75
Current residence: Lake Junaluska, NC
Occupation: Homemaker and Author

Lucy Neeley Adams and her husband, Woody, have been in the ministry for over fifty years in Middle Tennessee churches. They have also been missionaries in Korea and New Mexico and served on a college campus.

Their children, John, Scott, Ben, and Joy have blessed them with fourteen grandchildren and three great grandchildren. Lucy loves music and is the author of the book 52 Hymn Story Devotions. *Her website is www.52hymns.com.*

Religious Affiliation: Long's Chapel United Methodist Church.

Personal Scripture:

The thief cometh not, but for to steal and to kill and to destroy; I am come that they might have life and that they might have it more abundantly. *John 10:10 (KJV).*

REMEMBERING MY DADDY – WADSWORTH BURNSIDE NEELEY

September 23, 1890 – February 20, 1968

Lucy Neeley Adams

The last day I saw you, Daddy, you were in your hospital bed. That was an unlikely place for you to be because your life had been so full of manual labor. Your snow-white hair and your baby blue eyes reminded me of your very active years.

That busy life began quite early didn't it? As the oldest child you had to assume much responsibility at 12 years of age when your mother died. In fact, I believe your broken heart never really healed. Her pictures look lovely as well as loving and you were that special first child. Your father, who was very busy in his ministry at various churches, needed and trusted you to take care of your younger brother and two sisters.

Thank you for the many stories you told me. When you rode your horse, Dixie, to the neighbors' barns to pick up slop for the hogs, it must have been a terrible job. But the amazing experiences you told were always interesting. It was hard for you to tell about Dixie's death from "blind staggers."

I treasure the story of your receiving another horse that you trained. I never tired of the many times you recounted the history of your wonderful Prince Maxwell—"the horse that could see-saw, kneel down, get a shoe shine, and tell the time of day by your own watch." I usually saw a few tears in your eyes as you remembered that happiness.

But heartbreak became a part of your life again didn't it Daddy? There was a day you had to pack the show away and go back home, never to return to the bright lights of the stage and the applause. A big hole was left in your dreams but you did a wonderful thing when you got home. You came back and married your sweetheart, Louise, who became my mother and taught Prince another great accomplishment. Each day when you told him it was time to get the mail he trotted the short distance to the post office. The postman filled the bag you had placed in Prince's mouth, put it securely between his teeth again, and he trotted back home. After knocking on the door with his front hoof, he would deposit the bag at the door and return to the backyard.

My ears, my heart, and my wide eyes always spurred you on to "tell it again, Daddy, tell it again." You never refused any invitation to tell that story except when you were in the latter years and were afraid that you would cry. I imagine you heard many times during your childhood the untrue statement, "big boys don't cry."

Thank you for filling my dreams with those memories of yours. Thank you for the baseball games we attended together, the movies we went to, and the lemon ice cream we ate sitting at the table in Five Points. Thank you for letting me "go on the job" with you whether it was building, weather-stripping windows, or painting houses. I learned how to hammer a straight nail, how to use a screwdriver, and to sweep up the mess after sawing boards.

I am sorry that I was not an enthusiastic helper when I became a teenager. There were many new things on my mind. You remember that boyfriends became very important to me. You got angry at times but we usually worked through it.

So when I look at the little mountain summer home you built for our family at Lake Junaluska, I can see a few places where my handprints are evident. I love the places preserved in cement where we put the three leaves to represent the three ladies in your life, Mother, Margaret, and me. In fact, naming our cottage, "Mar-Luce" for us will always be a blessing from your loving heart.

Daddy, do you think that you pushed Margaret into performances with her singing and dramatic ability to fulfill your smashed dream of being on stage with your horse, Prince? Did you know that I wanted to be a star like the one you never got to be? Did you know that my dreams were frustrated because I didn't have the musical talent to do what Margaret did?

Now that I am older it is a huge blessing to know I only need to be who my heavenly

Father wants me to be. When I wrote about that in a brief devotional for the magazine *The Upper Room,* I was eager to show it to you the last time I saw you. It certainly brought laughter when you thought I had written the WHOLE magazine.

Age is a blessing when I remember my early years at home. I am thankful for a Daddy who loved me and protected me. I am grounded in the words that Jesus spoke to his disciples ...rejoice because your names are written in heaven. *Luke 10:20 (KJV).*

Since you, too, were assured of that promise, we will be together again someday—at home—our heavenly Home. My dearest daddy, I love you!

[This story first appeared as an article on June 15, 2011 in The Mountaineer of Waynesville, NC, where Lucy Adams was a guest columnist.]

REMEMBERING MY MOTHER – LOUISE BENNETT NEELEY

September 4, 1901 – April 17, 1990

Lucy Neeley Adams

The last day I saw you, Mother, you were in your hospital bed. I kept thinking it unbelievable that soon you would be moving into your heavenly home. Without words, your eyes spoke volumes of love for me. A single love-tear fell down your cheek. You wanted to speak but couldn't.

Did you feel the tear fall from your eye? Since you could not lift your hands to wipe it away, I immediately found a tissue to dry it. If I could re-live that day, I'd encourage you to let those tears flow as I hugged you and also shed my tears.

We never shared those moments of deep feeling did we? I saw no signs of weakness in you—only strengths because you wanted it that way. The message I received was that crying was weakness and I also must show strength, even if it was a mask that hid my hurts.

But, my dear mother, I am filled with some wonderful memories. Thank you for giving me birth. Thank you for making our home lovely and inviting.

Of all the childhood incidents, I remember a very special one when I was five. You were in shock when I picked our neighbor's beautiful iris to present to you — bulb and all. So together, we walked to her front door where I learned a difficult lesson in confession. As I held the flowers in my little hot hands you knocked on her door. With all the courage my five year old frame could hold, I whispered, "I am sorry, M-m-mrs. Going. Here a-a-a-re your flowers." I was quickly forgiven with a hug.

In my teen years my stuttering problems became unbearable. I couldn't speak in classes without fear of ridicule from other students. You heard my crying one night and comforted me. But you also began to study about speech problems and learned that stuttering can be the result of anxiety and tension. After a few visits with a friend who was a psychiatrist, he recognized that family conflicts and peer pressure had caused me to internalize a lot of stress and fear.

His suggestion was that I have a change of environment where I could finish school. So you and I moved to another town and eventually I stopped stuttering. We were amazed at my newfound freedom, which was wonderful! Without your courage to temporarily move from our home I may not have conquered that stutter. Thank you Mother, for your unselfishness and your strength to make that move for my sake.

During my college days and meeting Woody, the boy I chose to marry, it was a joy that you loved him like the son you never had. We were long time sweethearts but you never grew weary of his coming to the house, except the day you said, "Woody, why don't you go home and read a book so Lucy can bake a cake?" After our fifty-five years of a happy marriage, we remember that with a laugh. I think you were feeling the pain of my pulling away from home and expressed it with your humor.

In your later years, in spite of your painful arthritis, thank you for giving yourself, in great love and joy to my children. There is no way I could ever be a Nana like you were. The way they laughed at you and with you is a treasured memory. Your funny remarks, your unconditional love, and your never-ending patience are a precious part of their lives. I am grateful that you were their grandmother.

I have mentioned laughter several times. When I look through your 1922 Columbia College annual I read these words: "Lucy was unanimously voted the jolliest girl in our class." I also love to laugh so I must have inherited some of your "jolly genes."

As I grow older, I am well grounded in these words that Jesus spoke to his disciples. ...rejoice because your names are written in heaven. *Luke 10:20 (KJV).*

Since you were also assured of that promise, we will be together again someday— at home—our heavenly Home. My dearest mother, I love you!

[This story first appeared in the Mountaineer, Waynesville, NC, on May 2, 2006.]

A NOTE FROM THE AUTHOR: Background of the Remembering Stories.

If my mother and father were alive, I would treasure the time to share our loving experiences that I wrote about in the previous two stories. However, they have gone on to heaven and that is the reason I wrote about my remembering them. It was a joy to capture my thoughts and feelings of childhood. So, if it is possible, I urge the reader to share special memories now, with your parents. God bless you.

Marvel G. Adams

Year of birth: 1902
Age at writing: 90, now deceased

Occupation: Homemaker and Poet

Marvel Gossage Adams was born June 30, 1902 in Estil Springs, Tennessee. She died July 8, 1997. She was a marvelous minister's wife, mother, poet, and follower of Jesus Christ.

Religious Affiliation: United Methodist Church

THE FATHER'S HOUSE

Marvel G. Adams

There must be only a silvery mist between
This world and that other land unseen
Through which our loved ones pass, and
   disappear
From sight, but leave a lingering presence
   near.

Sometimes we stand beside a bed and hold
   the hand
Of one who soon is going to that land.
For just a fleeting moment, it seems we,
   too, can see
Beyond—and glimpse the joy that is to be.

And so we know that death is not a thing
   to fear,
But just a breath away from life, and very
   near
The Father's house, where one will find the
   door ajar
To enter home at last—it's not so far.

[Printed by permission from the author's family.]

CONSOLATION

Marvel G. Adams

Life just now is full of sorrows,
And of partings day by day;
We have fears for our tomorrows,
But we still can hope and pray.

Sometimes we cannot see through tears,
But we do have faith to know
That there is One who always hears
When, in grief, to Him we go.

He knows what courage it will take
When life's plans seem all undone;
He understands how hearts can ache—
For did He not give His Son?

We must still keep on believing
There's atonement in a Cross;
Despite these days of grieving,
There'll come joy—not all is loss.

[Printed by permission from the author's family.]

MY HOME

Marvel G. Adams

The Retirement Village is my home
And from this place I shall not roam.
Altho' I've moved from town to town
I now can change and settle down.

This is a special place to me
For we are one big family.
We share our joys and sorrows, too
And any trials we may pass through.

With staff and friends to help us out
Whenever there's a fear or doubt.
They are so patient and so kind
And never seem our needs to mind.

Sometimes we're tempted to complain
And it seems we cannot refrain
From worrying as we stand in line
Just waiting for the time to dine.

Of course we miss some of our youth,
And sometimes feel a little blue—
Until we realize and know,
There's not a better place to go.

[Printed by permission from the author's family.]

Woody A. Adams

Year of birth: 1933
Age at writing: 72
Current residence: Lake Junaluska, NC
Occupation: United Methodist Minister

I have been married for fifty-seven years to Lucy Neeley Adams and have four children, fourteen grandchildren, and three greats. I love to teach my Sunday school class, love to walk, and love to work in the yard.

Religious Affiliation: Long's Chapel United Methodist Church

Personal Scripture:

That at the name of Jesus every knee should bow, of things in heaven, and things in earth, and things under the earth; and that every tongue should confess that Jesus Christ is Lord, to the glory of God the Father.

Philippians 2:10–11 (KJV).

SAFELY BACK HOME

Read John 14:1–7

Woody Adams

Jesus said to [Thomas], "I am the way, and the truth, and the life." *John 14:6 (KJV).*

When I began my morning walk around the lake, I noticed that the fog was unusually heavy. I could hardly see ten feet in front of me. When the weather is clear, I can see buildings and homes and the sparkling waters of the lake. None of this was visible on this morning.

When I arrived on the opposite side of the lake, I looked out into the fog toward my home across the water. I could not see it, but I still knew it was there. I also knew that if I followed the walking path, I would arrive safely back home.

In our Christian walk, sometimes the hurts, fears, and frustrations of life are like the heavy fog. We cannot see our way clearly. But if we follow the path our Lord has laid out for us, we will arrive safely at our destination, a destination that brings healing and peace and joy.

And at the end of this life's walk, we are assured that Christ has prepared an eternal home for us where we will see him face to face. The fog will be lifted forever.

Prayer

O God, we thank you that in Jesus Christ we discover "the way, the truth, and the life."
Amen.

Thought for the day

Following the path God lays out will always lead us home.

Prayer Focus

Those searching for "the way home"

[This meditation originally published for use on 8/2/06 is reprinted from the Upper Room magazine, copyright by The Upper Room, Inc., P.O. Box 340004, Nashville, TN 37203–0004, and is used by permission of the publisher. Permission is required for all additional copying or use of this material.]

Margie Bender

Year of birth: 1938
Age at writing: 73
Current residence: Pace, FL
Occupation: Nurse

I am married with three children, one deceased, and seven grandchildren. My hobbies are drawing and knitting.

Religious Affiliation: Episcopal

Personal Scripture:

The LORD is my shepherd; I shall not want. He maketh me to lie down in green pastures: he leadeth me beside the still waters. He restoreth my soul: he leadeth me in the paths of righteousness for his name's sake. Yea, though I walk through the valley of the shadow of death, I will fear no evil: for though art with me; thy rod and thy staff they comfort me. Thou preparest a table before me in the presence of mine enemies: thou anointest my head with oil; my cup runneth over. Surely goodness and mercy shall follow me all the days of my life: and I will dwell in the house of the LORD for ever. *Psalm 23 (KJV).*

RENEWED FAITH

Margie Bender

Old I thought was a word for other people, not me. But when you retire you suddenly think, I must be getting old. I realize now the joy of getting old with God has always been there even before I retired.

Thinking of all the things God has created seems to become more realistic. Now I can enjoy waking up every day to hear the birds chirping and watch the squirrel I have named Rocky as he eats his corn. I can rock on the porch and enjoy the peace and quiet with the blue skies and mountains in the background. Raindrops on the roof are very relaxing.

I read that prayer is also part of growing old with God. Many years ago I really felt God did not hear any of my prayers. I prayed that he would not take my oldest boy from me after an auto accident, but he did. At that time I lost all faith in God when my son died. But as a nurse I was able to go on for the rest of my family.

I devoted more time to my nursing skills and helped families in their time of grief...just a silent prayer with them when they did not wish to talk.

My faith in God was restored over time as my grandchildren were born. Then I was blessed with meeting my high school sweetheart after fifty years. As we grow old together I know my faith in God has always been there. My high school sweetheart and I have now been married for 4 years. Each day is a blessing.

Now I know there is a joy to growing old with God.

Jackie Cobb

Year of birth: 1948
Age at writing: 64
Current residence: Gatlinburg, TN
Occupation: Computer programmer/database
   administrator

I have been married for twenty-three years to a sweet and caring man who is very supportive of me. Between us, we have four sons in their forties and two grandchildren. Both my husband and I retired from the U.S. Army Corps of Engineers in 2004 and relocated from Mississippi to the Great Smoky Mountains where we live today. In my spare time I enjoy crafts, sewing, keeping up with friends and family on Facebook, and reading. Visiting with the many friends I have made in the area is also a very enjoyable way to spend time.

Religious Affiliation: Episcopal

Personal Scriptures:

> Come unto me, all ye that labour and are heavy laden, and I will give you rest. Take my yoke upon you, and learn of me; for I am meek and lowly in heart: and ye shall find rest unto your souls. For my yoke is easy, and my burden is light.   *Matthew 11:28–30 (KJV).*

The Lord is my shepherd; I shall not want. He maketh me to lie down in green pastures; he leadeth me beside the still waters. He restoreth my soul; he leadeth me in the paths of righteousness for his name's sake. Yea, though I walk through the valley of the shadow of death, I will fear no evil; for thou art with me; thy rod and thy staff they comfort me.

Psalm 23:1–3 (KJV).

SIDE BY SIDE

Jackie Cobb

Even though I was not exposed to a life with God in it on a daily basis, I did have my grandparents to set the example of what it was like to live with God in your life. My father worked at a sawmill and died from an electrical accident when he was twenty-four. He died immediately, falling to the ground as my mother watched from a window in the small house where they lived. She was eight months pregnant with me.

After my father died, my mother moved in with her parents and I was born on Sunflower Plantation, near Drew, MS. My mother's parents were cotton sharecroppers and attended the Church of the Nazarene. They were very devout Christians and expected each of their thirteen children to be the same.

My mother married a violent alcoholic when I was two years old and during that marriage gave birth to five more children; two died at birth. One of the happiest days of my life was when she left my step-father when I was ten years old and moved back to Belzoni, MS near my father's parents.

My grandmother, "Mama Pool," and I became very close over the years. I was more fortunate than my siblings because of my close relationship with her; she was the most amazing person I have ever met.

It was because of "Mama Pool" that I began attending church, alone, when I was very young. She encouraged me, loved me, and gave me the strength and knowledge I needed to break out of the life my mother gave me. We attended church together when I visited her and she told me many times she would never have been able to overcome my father's death without God's help. She taught me that God helped her through the tough times and she was never alone, and that he would be with me too. I watched her grow old and experience many illnesses and despair when loved ones died, but she retained her joy because she grew old with God by her side. Right up until the time she died at age ninety-four, she always had a smile on her face and a kind word for everyone. I was blessed to have her in my life for so long and, even now, I miss her every day. I remember her teaching me to say my prayers and how to rely on God to support me during the tough times.

That happiness did not last long, my mother married again and had two more children; she married a total of eight times before dying at age seventy-two.

After leaving her parent's home my mother ceased attending church. Although she never forbade me to go, she would not go with me. She felt that throughout her childhood she had been forced to go to church, even when she didn't want to. Her father ruled his home with an iron hand and twisted the meaning of

32

Bible verses and used them in a frightening manner to threaten his children into submission to his will. Her mother taught her it was a sin to cut your hair, wear makeup, and dance. She felt there was no joy or happiness in church, only gloom and doom. Three years prior to her death she and her husband moved to his hometown in Mississippi. They began attending a Methodist church and both became very involved in it. She was finally able to hear the message of God as a blessing. She learned about forgiveness and how God loved her and could help her. She gave up drinking and lived her life as a testament to others.

When I was growing up, there were many nights I was alone and I prayed and asked God to let me know he was with me, and he always did.

I am now a sixty-four year old woman who has lived a life of violence, pain, rejection and poverty. I have suffered from the death of loved ones and undergone over twenty surgeries. I am fighting diabetes, high blood pressure, and high cholesterol as well as the incurable diseases of Meniere, Hypothyroidism, Sjogrens, and possibly Lupus. In spite of all this, I am truly happy and at peace because I know that I am not alone. I know that God is with me on this path of aging and deterioration. I know that I am truly growing old...side by side with Mama Pool and God.

Wayne Freeman

Year of birth: 1915
Age at writing: 95
Current residence: Maryville, TN
Occupation: Agricultural Research-Rice Breeding

I am widowed with three adult children; four grandchildren; and seven great grandchildren. I was raised on a farm in Kansas and attended Kansas State University and the University of Illinois where I received my MS and PHD Degrees. I began my career as a corn breeder at Mississippi State University, then the USDA in Tifton, GA, and a private company in Thomasville, GA. I went to India with the Rockefeller Foundation in 1961, first on Seeds for 5 years, then 10 years as Joint Coordinator, All India Rice Improvement Project, and then 15 years in Nepal as leader of the Integrated Cereals Project. I have served as member of the Board of Directors of the Barwale Research Foundation.

Religious Affiliation: Gatlinburg Presbyterian Church

Personal Scripture:

And God said let us make man in our image, after our likeness: and let them have dominion over the fish of the sea, and over the fowl of the air, and over the cattle, and over all the earth, and over ever creeping thing that creepeth upon the earth. So God created man in his own image, in the image of God created he him; male and female he created them.

Genesis 1:26–27 (KJV).

WHY DO WE LIVE?

Wayne Freeman

The Presbyterian denomination has a catechism question, "What is the chief end of man?" The answer to which is: "Glorify God and enjoy Him forever." This simple and yet profound answer is a political answer which one of my Indian friends explained, "Satisfies the questioner but provides no more information than when he asked the question."

In a retirement environment with the caregivers the only ones with a reasonable prospect of years of meaningful life, many of us many times may ponder the meaning of life in these circumstances. Over the years philosophers, theologians, and others have pondered the reason for life's existence. At our age and circumstances the answer to the question "What is the chief end of man?" deserves elaboration that is informative and rewarding—a guide to life in our twilight years. Some would say there is no answer, but attempts to provide answers have been many. Perhaps one of the best is Rick Warren's relatively recent book, *The Purpose Driven Life.*

What is the meaning of life? Warren has reviewed the written literature on the subject. One research project by Dr. Hugh Moorhead posed this question to 250 scientists, philosophers, intellectuals, and writers. Many posed the question back to Dr. Moorhead. Warren provides an answer to the seemingly insoluble question with a simple answer. It is "revelation." There are five purposes to life as revealed to us in God's written word brought to us over the centuries as recorded in our Holy Bible.*

Of immediate concern is our relationship to God. *Genesis 1:26, 27 (KJV)* simply states, Let us make man in Our image, according to Our Likeness...so God created man in His own image. Thomas Cahill elaborates on that relationship to bring humanity where it is today. Mankind has a self-value that lifts mankind from the status of a mere "primate" to man as a human that has a level of self-worth.

This self-value is best characterized as the human soul. In the view of the ancient Greeks and Romans human life was a cyclical affair that repeated itself from generation to generation. It was the value of the individual set forth in our Bible by the Hebrews that lifted mankind out of a cyclical existence to provide a level of self-esteem that enabled innovation and productivity that has enabled the development of modern industrial societies as we know them today. God as Creator enabled what we are today and it should be an eternal thanksgiving to God for what we were that enables what we are as a civilization today.

38

In summary, Warren says "We must begin with God, your Creator. You exist only because God wills that you exist. You were made by and for God, and until you understand that, life will never make sense. It is only in God that we discover our identity, our meaning, our purpose, our significance, and joy, and our destiny. Every other path leads to a dead end."

[Many may question Warren's analysis but he provides a perspective where for many, none existed before. And this could provide a good basis for why we live.]

Vern Hippensteal

Year of birth: 1948
Age at writing: 40
Current residence: Gatlinburg, TN
Occupation: Artist

I live in Gatlinburg with my wife Lisa. We run Hippensteal's Mountain View Inn. I try to paint watercolors daily. Our son, Woods, just graduated from the University of Tennessee with a degree in "Fine Art."

Religious affiliation: Methodist

Personal Scripture:

> For God so loved the world, that he gave his only begotten Son, that whosoever believeth in him should not perish, but have everlasting life. *John 3:16 (KJV)*

ABRAM'S FALLS

Vern Hippensteal

It has been said that raindrops
Are the tears of "God."
And rivers and creeks
Are the gathering of these tears.
If this is true
Then the waters that flow over Abram's Falls
Are from "His" tears of joy!

THE ANGEL OAK

Vern Hippensteal

You were old, when we were young,
a mighty fortress.
Our laughter rang as we played
beneath your branches.
We grew, and your leaves protected us
from the storms.
Wise, in solitude, you taught us to be
humble and patient.
Now, it is we, who are old and
still you are there for us.
In reverence you cradle us,
'til we are through.

Ron Lukat

Year of birth: 1947
Age at writing: 64
Current residence: Sevierville, TN
Occupation: Pastor of Gatlinburg Presbyterian Church

I am married to Barbara Lukat. I have two children and three grandchildren.

Religious Affiliation: Presbyterian

Personal Scripture:

Before I formed thee in the belly I knew thee; and before thou camest forth out of the womb I sanctified thee, and I ordained thee a prophet unto the nations. Then said I, Ah, Lord GOD! behold, I cannot speak: for I am a child.
Jeremiah 1:5–6 (KJV).

OLD AGE IS NOT FOR THE WEAK

Ron Lukat

My mother used to say as she got older that old age is not for the weak. She lived a good and healthy life until her last few years when heart failure finally took her life. I didn't fully appreciate the challenge of chronic illness that often accompanies many as they advance in age. The body doesn't always seem to keep up with the mind and spirit. At forty-five I encountered my first signs of heart trouble. Now at sixty-four, I have had three heart attacks and have fifteen stints in my heart. I haven't reached old age yet, but I have come to understand what my mother was talking about.

Faced by the reality of heart disease I have had to come to grips with my own mortality. I remember how after my first heart attack, I was shocked into the realization that I was not just going to get over this thing. The change of diet, the rehab, and the bouts of depression made me realize that every day of life is a gift from my Father in heaven, even if each day is accompanied by some adversities.

Being a pastor for thirty-four years, doing countless funerals, and talking to people about life and death and a relationship with God no doubt was helpful, but facing one's own mortality jumps across a great divide. I had to face the possibility of living and the possibility of dying. For me, the possibility of dying was not as difficult as the former. I had already come to trust the promises of Christ who assured me that He had gone on to prepare a place for me so that where he was I would be also. *John 14:3 (KJV)*. The prospect of leaving my wife and children certainly is not something I relish, but I am confident that their faith will sustain them when my time of passing comes. I have watched them by my bedside numerous times as they have taken me in for heart caths, and tried to reassure me as I writhed in pain with another blockage or heart attack. I am sure that they have come to grips with the possibility of my passing. They know I love them and am doing everything I can to put off the inevitable. As much as I have tried to provide for them in the eventuality of my death, I know and they know that it will not be how I have provided for them, but how God will provide for them that will really sustain them. Time and again, we have had to trust God to see us through the crises of life, and God has never failed to open doors when it was needed, give hope when all looked so bleak, or carried us when things were so difficult that we did not even have words to pray.

What I look forward to is that time when all suffering and sorrow will cease and all things will be redeemed and reconciled to God. *Revelation 21:4 (KJV)*. I look forward to when I will finally be able to see God face to face and bask in the full radiance of his glory as did the disciples on the Mount of Transfiguration *(Matthew 17)*. I don't know exactly what heaven is going to look like but I do believe that it will be glorious and that I will be reunited with all those I have loved and who have been so instrumental in my faith and relationship with God.

There have been several times when I sat with great Christians of faith who were facing imminent death and felt free enough to talk with me about what they were experiencing and expecting. I remember sitting with my mother-in-law when she looked up toward the ceiling and said, "Ron, what is that bright shining city I see. It is glorious." "It is the new Jerusalem," I said. Not long afterward, she passed on. I don't have any scientific explanation of what she saw and I am sure many would just pass it off as a delusion, but my faith tells me that for her it was a vision of what God had in store for her and what John talked about in the book of Revelation. I sat with others who sang hymns and talked about that glorious time when we would finally be with our Lord. The joy with which they looked forward to the fulfillment of their hopes and faith helps me look forward to what is to come. When I leave this world, don't cry for me. I know that my greatest hopes and dreams will be realized and nothing but peace will fill my soul.

The greater challenge for me has been the possibility of living. I want my life to count for something. I want it to honor God. I firmly believe that the purpose of my being is to glorify God and enjoy him forever. That is the first question of the Westminster Catechism I learned as a child. Trying to figure out what that means and how I do that has been a life-long pursuit. Faced with the prospect of not being able to do that with all my youthful health and energy has required a whole new perspective as I advance toward "old" age.

Wanting my life to count for something means that what I have done and witnessed to will be worth remembering. I know that we are but fading flowers and that all things in this mortal world in time will pass. However, I do believe that if I can connect with something immortal that my life will have counted for something. The only thing immortal and unchanging is God. Therefore my witness to God and work in His Kingdom gives me the opportunity to have my life count for something immortal, and lasting, and meaningful.

For several years now the doctors have advised me to retire and take it easy. I certainly don't want to be foolish about what I do, but neither do I want to cease living life to the fullest and living every day as if it were the last opportunity I will have to show forth the glory of God and the joy I have in His blessings that are being poured out in my life. Too much time spent navel gazing or in idle pursuits has a tendency to turn my attention on myself and away from serving God. When God called me to lay down my nets and come and follow him into the ministry, I committed myself to letting God make the decisions as to where I would go and what I would do. This has given me a freedom to not blame myself for the failures to accomplish everything I envisioned for my life, and the humility to not give myself too much credit for my successes. I trust in God instead to give me life each day and to fill it with joy and peace. With that I am content.

Teri Pizza

Year of birth: 1947
Age at writing: 64
Current residence: Gatlinburg, TN
Occupation: Retired Realtor

I count as my greatest achievements my marriage of nearly forty years, my two children, and the four grandchildren they have given me. I like to read, write, and garden.

Religious Affiliation: Episcopal

Personal Scripture:

Be still, and know that I am God.
Psalm 46:10 (KJV).

RE: GOD

Teri Pizza

Years have gone by and I have entered into my old age. The joy is that I am finding out more about my Resurrected God. Consequently, I am learning that old age is just a vehicle toward knowing my Lord, my Master, my Teacher.

He is about repair and renewal, restoration and reliance, refreshment and recreation. He is the reason for reconstructed lives, revived relationships, and redirected energies. He allows us to be recognized, regenerated, and rehabilitated. He is a remarkable and reliable God.

And, no matter what age His children may be; no matter what has transpired in our lives, He is relevant. No matter how far or how often we have turned away from Him, He is always ready to assure us that there is nothing man has done that God can't RE-DO & REDEEM!

> For I am persuaded, that neither death, nor life, nor angels, no principalities, nor powers, nor things present, nor things to come, nor heights, nor depth, nor any other creature shall be able to separate us from the love of God which is in Christ Jesus our Lord.
>
> *Romans 8:38–39 (KJV).*

GOD'S GIFT

Teri Pizza

As I grow older, I am grateful for much, but mostly for the wisdom God has given me regarding weakness. Who would have thought of calling weakness a gift? Not just a gift, but a great gift? I wouldn't have and I bet you wouldn't have either. However, I am here to tell you just that.

As it turns out, weakness is one of God's riddles, paradoxes, conundrums, and proof that God is not only generous, but also, for me, seems to have a most wonderful, quirky sense of humor.

Many, many times I have finally given up and said something like, "God, I have done all I can think of doing and I can't go any further with this. I just give up." Then, low and behold and to my surprise and utter delight, He comes to my rescue. Just when I'm ready to give up, He gives me the solution, fixes the problem, or sends the right person. All because I quit being "strong;" because I admitted my weakness and His omnipotence. I simply get so exhausted trying to fix it on my own (my way) that I have to let go, to let Him be God, and I rely on His strength. I can almost see Him smiling when this happens with an almost "I told you so" grin upon his heavenly face. He loves doing, fixing, making things right for us. He loves it when He knows, "we get it."

Why should we be surprised? As with so many of God's paradoxes, like the last shall be first, men must become like children, and we need to be reborn; Christ demonstrated this phenomenon of reversal or heavenly thinking over and over during His lifetime. He cleansed the unclean leper, gave us the parable about the father celebrating rather than chastising the prodigal son. Even with Peter, as Peter protested that he would never betray Him and yet did over and over and over, even then, God accepted Peter's weakness and made a rock out of him upon which God built His church. I am utterly amazed at the outstanding love of our Lord and Savior.

Now, I relish the aging because, as I do, I rely more upon Him to teach me, to help me, to provide for me. And, because He is faithful to do all of that and more, I am able to live a bigger and better life...a life of spirit...a life of joy. For instance, I have retired to a community far removed from my children and grandchildren and longtime friends, giving me lots of hours to miss them, but God fills those empty hours teaching me more about Him as I read His book. He brings into my life people I would have never spent extended time with in the past. He shows me that I need to see Him in everyone and they delight me. He has given me ministries that I never would have picked for myself and has stretched my mind and my abilities. He has surrounded me with the Great Smoky Mountains, again reminding me to look and see His whole creation and how He has wondrously woven it all together for the benefit of us earthly creatures.

Constantly I see God's love for everyone and His great desire to teach us to love each other. My days fill up and fly by quickly doing and being His disciple. But, in order to learn the lessons I have had to allow myself to be weak, to be more humble, to acknowledge His strength. Then and only then can He act, give, bless, sanctify.

So, I have become most grateful for this special gift of old age, time, and knowledge given to me by the One who can turn night into day, oceans into dry land, and hate into love. I more fully understand Paul when he tells the Philippian church,

> Brethren,...this one thing I do, forgetting those things which are behind, and reaching forth unto those things which are before, I press toward the mark for the prize of the high calling of God in Christ Jesus.
> *Philippians 3:13–14 (KJV).*

My prayer and my hope is that my children and my children's children will learn this lesson earlier than I; and, eagerly embrace age, even as it weakens bodies, as an opportunity to find out more about God whose strength and love can always be relied upon.

Because the foolishness of God is wiser than men; and the weakness of God is stronger than men. For ye see your calling, brethren, how that not many wise men after the flesh, not many mighty, not many noble, are called: But God hath chosen the foolish things of the world to confound the wise; and God hath chosen the weak things of the world to confound the things which are mighty.

I Corinthians 1:25–27 (KJV).

Alta Chase Raper

Year of birth: 1940
Age at writing: 70–71
Current residence: Sevierville, TN
Occupation: United Methodist minister

I am a widow with four children, seven grand-children, and one great grandson. I love to read and write stories and articles.

Religious Affiliation: United Methodist, Pittman Center Circuit.

Personal Scripture:

And we know that all things work together for good to them that love God, to them who are the called according to his purpose.
Romans 8:28 (KJV).

THE PASTOR'S PONDERINGS OF JUNE 20, 2004

Alta Chase Raper

In clearing out the overgrowth of trees around the parsonage, a set of old concrete steps was uncovered down near the end of our driveway. They have caused me to ponder on the Pittman Center of long ago; little barefoot children and grown-ups alike, with emotionless faces, trudging up the hill to the infirmary which was then located right here where the parsonage now stands. All of them, coming to see old Doc Thomas, who could fix most anything that ailed you. When the visits here slowed a mite, you could see 'ole Doc' riding his horse all over these hills and valleys; birthing the babies (human and otherwise), pulling teeth, and calming the fever. "Twarn't nothin' fer him to even doctor yore old horse, or yore cow, if'n it was ailin'." Lo, the many years he served here as doctor, dentist, veterinarian, preacher, and friend. Why, he even delivered Dolly Parton herself, and likely some of her other eleven brothers and sisters!

Established by the New York District of the Methodist Church through the efforts of Eli Pittman and John Burnett, this was a highly populated and bustling mission town in the early 1900s. I would think it was much like our present day, Red Bird Mission or Henderson Settlement. Jobs were created, skills were taught and learned, and every Sunday, the Glory of the Lord came down with old-time preachin', prayin', and singin'. And, when you got to marrying age...church was the best courtin' place you could find anywhere. Sitting on the back pew holding hands, or on the long walk home in the dark of the evening when you could 'steal a little sugar' from your sweetheart's cheek.

If those *old steps* could talk...they would tell of the strong faith, yet meager existence of these mountain folks who worked hard to provide for their families and to care for each other. The first school in Pittman Center was a most welcome sight! Children of all ages and sizes were brought in by horseback and wagon, to partake in the opportunity of an education.

In late evening, loud claps of thunder, flashing lightning, and downpours of rain frequented the mountains. I can just see the women now, gathering up the children and hurrying to the middle of the 'feather bed' for safety from the lightning. Mothers in aprons, scurrying around the old wood stove preparing cornmeal mush, fried taters, or pinto beans. Dads coming in from the fields, dirty from a day's work; making a beeline down to the creek to wash up before supper time. Oh, what tales they would tell...if those old steps could talk! Our fathers have told us what you did in their days, in days long ago. *Psalm 44:1 (KJV).*

THE PASTOR'S PONDERINGS OF JULY 16, 2006

Alta Chase Raper

We all have our moments of pure grace, moments of sweet delight, special moments when we feel God with us, oh, so intimately. In times like these, I get chills as I literally feel Him wrapping invisible arms around me, encircling me with unconditional love. And He invites me to accept His presence. My heart seems to settle somewhere in my throat and I am amazed at the awesomeness of Almighty God; the Creator of all that is and ever shall be.

There are so many ways I experience true communion with God. Like the week we were in Myrtle Beach; I saw a rainbow and thought it had to be the most beautiful I had ever seen. When I looked again, there was a second rainbow right beside the first! And I thought of God reassuring me, twice over, of His great love and mercy. Never before have I seen two rainbows, side by side with colors so vibrant! Each one clearly defined; violet, aqua, pink, and yellow; so magnificent that praises deep within me bubbled up and escaped my lips! And the bow shall be in the cloud; and I will look upon it, that I may remember the everlasting covenant between God and every living creature of all flesh that is upon the earth. *Genesis 9:16 (KJV)*.

God's presence is so real in the gurgling of a clear mountain stream; in a cool gentle breeze on a hot summer day; in a bird's warble or the chatter of squirrels high in the old oak tree in our front yard. God speaks to me when I find a shiny new penny in an unusual place...and I am reminded "in God we trust." When I see our American flag fully unfurled in the wind, I think of freedom and my heart is glad! I am grateful to those who fought and died on foreign soil so that we might live here in peace. I think of those blessed to return home from war to loved ones who can never comprehend the magnitude of all these soldiers have seen and done. And I think of my earthly father and the goodness of God in keeping him safe during WWII and the time he endured in the belly of a great ship in the Pacific Ocean. Thanks be to God! He gives us the victory through our Lord Jesus Christ. *I Corinthians 15:57 (KJV)*.

God speaks to me in the soothing refrain of a great old hymn of the church, and I'm reminded of Charles Wesley as I try to imagine the passion he must have felt as he penned such beautiful words of praise and honor. *Sing to the Lord a new song; sing to the Lord, all the earth. Psalm 96:1 (KJV)*.

I see God's eyes in the eyes of a caring friend and I feel His touch in their embrace. He joins me in laughter; and in my tears, He feels my pain. I know that everything is in order as He tells me, *There is a time to weep and* a time to laugh, a time to mourn and a time to dance, a time to embrace and a time to refrain, a time to search and a time to give up, a time for war and a time for peace... *Ecclesiastes 3 (KJV)*, and I feel His presence. And I know I am loved For God so loved the world that He gave His Son that the world through Him might be saved. *(John 3:16)* God has made known to me the path of life; and he fills me with joy in His presence.

Be assured that we, His children, shall be kept "as the apple of His eye; and hidden in the shadow of His wings from the wicked who assail us." May God bless you today and everyday with the little things of life that bring you fully into His Holy presence.

THE PASTOR'S PONDERINGS OF MAY 2, 2010

Alta Chase Raper

Good morning! What a beautiful Lord's Day...they are all beautiful to me! I can think of nothing better than getting up every morning in beautiful Pittman Center, Tennessee. I've told you before I am so blessed that God, the Bishop, and the District Superintendent appointed me to this charge almost ten years ago. I have loved every minute of it!

Let me tell you about yesterday morning! Once again my mother and I were invited guests of the Pittman Center Class of 1949's Annual Breakfast hosted by Blanche Moyers. We had the best time! Eating good food and listening to funny stories is about as good as it gets. I just sat back and listened...

"Remember when I finally got out of the algebra class? I went down by the creek and I burned that book! I hated algebra!"

"Oh, and do you remember Ms. _____? She was a nervous sort wasn't she? Remember every time we would act up, she would say, 'Now children, straighten up or we will have to pray.'"

"Do you know our class is the only one that still has an annual meeting? There were twenty of us in the graduating class and seven of us are here this morning!" (Whereupon, Mayor Glenn Cardwell, a member of the class, read the roll of the deceased members and each one who was absent was recognized and remembered.)

Mom and I sat next to Ruby who had us in stitches when she told about the boy who sat behind her who undid the sash to her dress and tied her to the back of the chair during class. When class was over, she couldn't get up.... I laughed so hard as I mentally pictured this scene.

"Remember our principal, Dr. Quigley? Lord, have mercy! I was scared to death of that man!" and on and on...wish I had more time to tell you more stories this morning but I better get crackin'. It is time to get ready for church!

Before we left, I was duly sworn in by Mayor Glenn as an honorary member of the "Class of 49" and officially became a "Forty-Niner." What a delightful morning and one I shall long remember.

Memories, passed along to each generation by the elders, keep our history alive. The land and its people will live on in the hearts and minds of those who care to listen, remember, and pass them on to the next generation.

What may seem mundane and insignificant now, will someday be recalled as a 'remember when' becoming the source of many conversations and thoughts as we grow older...sitting on the front porch in an old swing or rocking chair; talking and laughing, as we, too, recall days gone by.

There is another time when it is important to listen, listen very closely, and learn...to that still small voice of God. In order to hear him we must be quiet. Be still, and know that I am God. *Psalm 46:10 (KJV)*. Do you ever feel guilty when you hear that verse? There are times when guilt almost overwhelms me. *James 1:19 (KJV)* speaks also of hearing, Wherefore, my beloved brethren, let every man be swift to hear, slow to speak, slow to wrath: Listen! Can you hear Him?

THE PASTOR'S PONDERINGS OF JANUARY 8, 2012

Alta Chase Raper

When I awaken to the cold crispness of the early dawn, the first image I see outside my window is the trees on the mountainside, sometimes wet and dripping from a nighttime shower and sometimes clothed in the sparkling icy frost of the night before. And I ponder on these trees. How they have a story all their own; a story of constant change, of beauty and plainness, of growth and rest... and all of it so very closely paralleling our own.

As now, in the dead of winter their stark nakedness reveals dark silhouettes of aged trees, skeleton like figures with grotesque arms reaching in all directions with trunks bent and branches gnarled and broken. Younger trees stand tall boasting straight trunks and graceful branches like the outstretched arms of the lithesome, effortless grace of a ballerina. On the outside, they all appear dormant, barren, and defenseless; but on the inside, there is still the sweet sap of life itself waiting for God's call to "wake up!"

Spring will bring the trees out of their deep sleep, clothing them in the delicate 'spring green' of new life. Ah, so beautiful!

Tiny, coiled leaves emerge from the pregnant branches, as wee buds begin to form and decorate the trees with the first hint of flowering fruition. Bugs and worms sometimes invade trees left to themselves; but with nurture and care, they evolve into the magnificent splendor of nature's intention.

Summer finds the trees filled with spontaneity, maturity, and provision. Almost overnight, they seem to burst forth, robed in their finest array. Luscious foliage, flowers, and fruit clothe them in unimaginable splendor. They preen and boast while providing shade from the heat and rest for the weary who languish beneath their branches. Children climb their sturdy limbs to seek adventure while passing the lazy summer days. Their fruit provides nourishment as it is savored, enjoyed, and even preserved for the days and months ahead.

Fall brings rest and a slowing down time as the trees prepare for another long winter's nap. Their dark green foliage turns to vibrant reds, yellow, and gold. They look forward to turning inward once again when the gusty winds and pounding rain bring their colorful clothing to rest on the ground to return again from whence it came.

So are the seasons of our lives. We are born, we live, and then we die, to bloom again in God's own fields. Listen to these words from the book of Ecclesiastes, which reveals the very meaning of life, even as it is questioned. He has made everything beautiful in its time. *Ecclesiastes 3:11 (KJV)*.

Helen Hughes Rice

Year of birth: 1923
Age at writing: 88
Current residence: Waynesville, NC
Occupation: Teacher (retired)

I was born in Dunn, NC. My first husband was Reverend Miles Preston Hughes, Jr. (AL). I am a mother of five children, nine grandchildren and two great grandchildren. My hobbies are writing, bridge, autoharp, piano, knitting, scrapbooking, poetry. My second husband is Wayne Kendall Rice (IN).

Religious Affiliation: United Methodist

Personal Scripture:

Sermon on the Mount.   *Matthew 5–7 (KJV)*.

Judge not, that ye be not judged. For with what judgment ye judge, ye shall be judged: and with what measure ye mete, it shall be measured to you again.   *Matthew 7:1–2 (KJV)*.

THROUGH IT ALL...

Helen Hughes Rice

Through It all...
I've tried to
stand tall,
Knowing others
have the same obsession
To make an
acceptable impression...
All the time
feeling vulnerable and meek...
Realizing
others are better, so to speak.
But leaning on
the Lord all the while
Trying to convey
love with a smile...
What does the
Lord require of thee?
"To do justly,
love mercy and walk humbly"
With help from
the Almighty above,
Through it all,
to simply LOVE!

WHO AM I? WHERE HAVE I BEEN?

Helen Hughes Rice

At 88 it's been a whirlwind!
The 1st 20 years, raised in a happy home.
The 2nd 20 years, a parsonage home of my
    own.
Widowed at 50, I had to stay "nifty"
For the 3rd 20 years—
A teaching career.
The 4th 20 years, a 2nd marriage with some
    tears—But happy travels, happy step-
    family, but Wayne's declining health,
His long illness, ending in death.
So, in these 5th 20 years, what lies ahead?
With the presence of God, I need not dread
My own failing health, leading to death.
I praise the Almighty for each precious day.
I stay close to Him to live life His way—
    Remembering
The love of two husbands and hundreds of
    kin,
My own five children, their spouses, nine
    "grand,"
Helping educate them or any way I can,
Grateful for who I am, and where I have been!

Nancy Richards

Year of birth: 1946
Age at writing: 65
Current residence: Gatlinburg, TN and Suba,
  Kenya
Occupation: Missionary with Kenya Islands
  Missions, Inc., a Tennessee 501c3 corp-
  oration, registered in Kenya as the NGO
  Suba Environmental Education of Kenya.

I am married to Don Richards, my missionary
partner, whom I met in the Amazon jungle, and
author of "Mission Wild." We seek the
transformation of greater Suba (Kenya), the
poorest and most HIV + district in the country,
by providing opportunities for young and old to
know God through the wonders of His creation,
while becoming environmentally literate, able to
address environmental issues in a Biblical way
that cares for both people and the earth.

Personal Scripture:

And the Lord God took the man and put him
into the Garden of Eden to dress it and to keep
it.   *Genesis 2:15 (KJV).*

For by him were all things created, that are in
heaven, and that are in earth, visible and
invisible, whether they be thrones, or

dominions, or principalities, or power: all things were created by him, and for him.

Colossians 1:16 (KJV).

And—*Isaiah 61.*

BUT THE RIGHTEOUS WILL LIVE BY HIS FAITH.

HABBAKUK 2:4

Nancy Richards

Dear Friends and Family,

We feel God has been showing us He can meet our needs and enable us to go forward in these times.

With the economy struggling, people are not feeling able to give as before, and the amount of money coming in for our ministry and for others has decreased. So much thanks to you who are faithfully continuing to give!

This past few months for us getting food to eat, gas for our car, and paying bills have become things we have not taken for granted. Instead of money coming the usual way, we have seen direct individual acts of kindness, teaching us to look beyond the regular ways of support. An example, one time when we were out of food, my brother Sam and his wife Regina showed up at the door all the way from Alabama and made gallons of the best gourmet Brunswick Stew you ever put in your mouth. We agreed this was our manna— perhaps a bit tastier.

Another time we received a Kroger card for $100 from a friend who said the Lord spoke to her in the laundromat to send that exact amount for that store. Another friend provided toothpaste, soap, etc.

The son of our pastor in Kenya sent us a BP gas card. We used it to travel to speak at a church. A youth group took up an offering for us when Don shared with them, enabling us to purchase vitamins for our seven months in Kenya. (Vitamins in Kenya are outrageously expensive, and we do a lot better at survival with vitamins.)

A dear one sent a gift certificate to Cold Water Creek, and I was able to purchase something to look more dignified in Kenya. A Christmas gift from our son and his wife gave me something nice to wear in church.

Our son in LA and his new wife paid for us to change our air tickets so we could spend a bit more time with them...and the airlines decided to only charge for one ticket.

We are bathed in the blessings of peoples' kindnesses, too many to report. In *Matthew 11:28* Jesus tells us that He takes away the burden and refreshes us with rest! God declares to Jeremiah who is in prison, Call unto Me and I will answer you and show you great and mighty things that you know not. Our part? To come to Jesus and let Him lift our burdens and to call to God expectantly. To walk alongside Him in His service.

This past month as we prepared to leave for Africa on Tuesday, February 21st, we listed the bills and the needs for the trip and listed the money that had come in. They didn't match! But a reminder of *Philippians 4:19* glided into our minds: ...my God will supply all your need according to his riches in glory in Christ Jesus. What happened? We spoke to God of our trust in Him and believed this Word, and though we couldn't see how, we knew He would meet all our needs.

> ➢ A dear saint offered to pay for our airfare to Kenya via South Africa, where God had encouraged us to go to visit Don's son whom we haven't seen in two years.
> ➢ Don's son paid for our stay in a B&B near his home.
> ➢ A friend offered to pick us up at the airport and lend us a car.
> ➢ For our board meeting, two members slipped us traveling money and looked after our accommodation. Another fixed a meal for the meeting. *Our laptop crashed!* Jamie and Whit Gilbert presented us with a beautiful top of the line laptop that Whit had won as a prize...never been opened or turned on!
> ➢ The computer guy who pronounced the diagnosis on our old laptop and took out its brain, installed it into the new one, and as I reach for my checkbook said, "Just take it. I didn't do much."
> ➢ I went to get a haircut from the best stylist around, a haircut that would last. "I just want to give this to you," she said, "I have been so blessed lately."

➤ We had budgeted tightly for seven months of blood pressure medicine. The dear doctor at Mountain Hope Good Shepherd Clinic paid for Don's medicine.

➤ And so exciting, Don at 81 years of age, last year having been diagnosed with a slow growing prostate cancer, has just come back from the clinic after a comprehensive blood test with a clean bill of health, the best shape he has ever been in!

We are so grateful! And to many more, too numerous to list.

What Jesus accomplished at the cross is way past what we can fathom, and it is powerful. *His Kingdom is heaven on earth.* He paid for it. It is ours. We seek Him and ask for wisdom as we are in His word, and whatever He shows us, we are to hold on to, like soil to a seed till we see it come forth. There is a gestation period, but the baby will come! We are to exercise our authority over hard things, proclaiming His Word until we see it, see widows and the orphans basking in His undying love and cared for in necessities. What He calls us to will come to pass if we count the cost and pay it, the cost of laying down our lives for those He loves. *Luke 14:25–35.*

[From Don and Nancy Richards' February 2012 Kenya Islands Missions, Inc. Email Newsletter.]

H. Alvin Sharpe

Year of birth: 1910
Age at writing: 65, now deceased
Occupation: Artist/author

*He was born in a log cabin in Jacks Fork, KY.
He had one child, six grandchildren, nine great
grandchildren, and two great-great grandchildren. He was a marine artist, engraver
Intaglio process (etchings), jewelry designer,
ship captain, creator of the Rex doubloon,
several art series produced by Hamilton mint,
and prospector.*

*Religious Affiliation: Methodist and avid reader
of the Bible*

Personal Scripture:

The Lord is my light and my salvation; whom
shall I fear? The Lord is the strength of my life;
of whom shall I be afraid?   *Psalm 27:1 (KJV).*

TEN TALBAS'A

H. Alvin Sharpe

I believe in a God universal,
Omnipotent in life, space and time.
His goodness encompassing and ageless,
This God, this God of mine.

And ours a single obligation
(We are His potters at hand)
To shape our life (His vessel)
And place upon it His brand.

I believe every living creature
To be a cellular part of Him,
And in His final purpose
To be the whole of them.

I believe in a God generous,
Tho measuring all for worth
When He gave life to the waters
And light to benighted Earth.

I believe reward and punishment
(Self "seeding" by Divine Plan)
Proclaim before creation
His emancipation of man.

I believe in a God of wisdom
Meting justice to all men.
When we choose to give Him reason
His choice is how, and when.

I believe in a God, our Father,
Forbearing and patient of whim
On the part of His "wayward" children
Ordain'd in His image by Him.
I believe in a God of compassion,
Divine in life, time and space,
Who calls in time His servants
To stand before Him face to face.
I believe in a God creative,
Who allots His labors divine.
Yet, He gives no overburden,
This God, this God of mine.

I believe in a life everlasting
To begin on Judgment Day,
And I fear no scourge or evil,
If I live this one His way.

[From the author's book, *Collected Meditations.* Reprinted
with permission from the author's daughter, Lynn Sharpe
Celestin.]

MEDITATION AT "JACOB'S CHAIR"

SAN JUAN CO., UTAH

H. Alvin Sharpe

I come here with troubled heart
...and harassed mind,
To rest yet, a while,
With my feet in the rubble
Of a hundred million years.

I survey around me
The vastness of His creation,
The infinity of His space,
The eternity of His time.

I measure now by these criteria
The breadth of my vanities,
My passions and my greeds,
As well as the depth
Of a selfish, shallow mind.

When I have done these measures,
I will leave in humility,
Let these proofs find me wanting
In His image, and lost forever
From His presence
Eternal, omnipotent, divine.

[From the author's book, *Collected Meditations*. Reprinted with permission of the author's daughter, Lynn Sharpe Celestin.]

MEDITATION AT THE TOMB OF THE UNKNOWN SOLDIER

H. Alvin Sharpe

Eternal God of justice and wisdom,
Omnipotent—over life, land, and sea,
Resting here at your divine mercy,
Lies a flower—that hath fallen a'lee.
In noble defense—of his country,
When beckon'd, he answered the call.
While we the living gave so little,
We asked of him—his all.
That his gift be not wantonly wasted,
Dear Lord, we ask that this be
A beacon and shrine of peace forever,
This tomb of a "flower" fallen a'lee.
We know not how men you measure,
But he stood in the shoes of the tall.
While we living boasted our "little,"
He stepped forth, and gave—his all.
So, God of our Fathers,—a blessing.
Unto your Kingdom, give the key
To this the most generous of givers
Who lies here—"fallen, a'lee."
If in right—we decorate the living,
How then—can the fallen we pay?
For his repose—in Abraham's bosom,
Dear God—we fervently pray.
Tho forever to us he is nameless,

Please, God, we ask it of thee,
Let bloom again—in thy garden,
This "flower that hath fallen a'lee."

[Reprinted with permission from the author's daughter, Lynn Sharpe Celestin.]

Faye Jean Warriner

Year of birth: 1930
Age at writing: 81
Residence: Plainfield, IN
Occupation: Retired secretary

I have been a widow for nine years. I am kept busy helping older senior citizens taking care of their medical information and funeral affairs.

Religious Affiliation: Plainfield United Methodist Church

Personal Scripture:

But thou, when thou prayest, enter into thy closet, and when thou hast shut thy door, pray to thy Father which is in secret; and thy Father which seeth in secret shall reward thee openly.
Matthew 6:6 (KJV).

BEDTIME THOUGHTS...

Faye Jean Warriner

You know what? I might take my tape recorder to bed some night, just so you could hear my prayers and talks with God. I really believe He must think I am "goofy" because of some of the things I talk to Him about...*but I know He is the one person I have always and can always turn to!*

[An email to the compilers of this book as she regretfully turned down the invitation to submit her story of her walk with God! Can you "hear" the joy?]

INDEX BY TITLE

Abram's Falls 43

The Angel Oak 45

Bedtime Thoughts 99

But the Righteous Will Live By His Faith 85

Consolation 17

The Father's House 15

God's Gift 59

Meditation at "Jacob's Chair" 93

Meditation at the Tomb of the Unknown Soldier 95

My Home 19

Old Age is Not for the Weak 49

The Pastor's Ponderings of June 20, 2004 65

The Pastor's Ponderings of July 16, 2006 67

The Pastor's Ponderings of May 2, 2010 71

The Pastor's Ponderings of January 8, 2012 75

Re: God 57

Remembering My Daddy 5

Remembering My Mother 9

Renewed Faith 27

Safely Back Home 23

Side by Side 31

Ten Talbas'a 91

Through It All 79

Who Am I? Where Have I Been? 81

Why Do We Live? 37

CPSIA information can be obtained
at www.ICGtesting.com
Printed in the USA
FFOW02n1924220816
26914FF